Before They Were Famous

Teddy Roosevelt

Written by Stephen Krensky
Illustrated by Bobbie Houser

A Crabtree Crown Book

CRABTREE
Publishing Company
www.crabtreebooks.com

School-to-Home Support for Caregivers and Teachers

This appealing book is designed to teach students about core subject areas. Students will build upon what they already know about the subject, and engage in topics that they want to learn more about. Here are a few guiding questions to help readers build their comprehension skills. Possible answers appear here in red.

Before Reading:

What do I know about this topic?

- *I know that Teddy Roosevelt was a president of the United States.*
- *I know that Teddy Roosevelt was a member of the Rough Riders and went to Cuba during the Spanish-American War.*

What do I want to learn about this topic?

- *I want to learn what type of exercises Teddy did when he was young to get stronger.*
- *I want to learn how many years Teddy Roosevelt was president.*

During Reading:

I'm curious to know...

- *I'm curious to know why Teddy Roosevelt enjoyed being a hunter and killing animals.*
- *I'm curious to know how old Teddy was when he first went to the Dakota Territory to hunt bison.*

How is this like something I already know?

- *It is well known that Teddy Roosevelt loved the outdoors and wanted to preserve large tracts of land for future generations.*
- *I know that Teddy Roosevelt started many conservation projects, including the National Park Service.*

After Reading:

What was the author trying to teach me?

- *I think the author wanted to show that in addition to being the president in Washington D.C., Teddy Roosevelt was also a great outdoorsman.*
- *The author explained that being weak and sickly as a child prompted Teddy to work hard to get stronger physically and mentally.*

How did the photographs and captions help me understand more?

- *I found the photographs gave me an excellent idea of how strong and capable Teddy Roosevelt became while a young man.*
- *I liked learning that Teddy Roosevelt owned a 218-acre (88-hectare) ranch that later became a part of the Little Missouri National Grassland.*

Table of Contents

Heading West

Teddy Roosevelt did not exactly look like a cowboy. True, he was wearing the right clothes. And he had a **lasso** and a rifle. Most importantly, he was riding a horse.

But he didn't look comfortable. Not yet.

Fun Facts

Teddy Roosevelt first headed west to the Dakota Territory, now North Dakota and South Dakota, in 1883 to hunt with his brother, Elliott.

The Dakota Territory was still part of the **Wild West** in 1883. It wasn't an easy place to fit in. When Teddy first arrived, local people laughed at him behind his back.

Clearly, he was just a **city slicker** from New York City, someone who wanted to play for a little while in the big western sandbox.

Fun Facts

While over 100,000 people lived in the Dakota Territory in the 1880s, about 2 million lived in New York City at the same time.

Getting Stronger

But Teddy was tougher than he looked. As a young boy he had suffered from nightmares because he had so much trouble breathing. He was weak and skinny and got tired easily. One time, in fact, two older boys roughed him up a bit without even trying.

Teddy hated being picked on. But what could he do about it?

"Theodore," said his father, Theodore Roosevelt Sr. "You have the mind but you have not the body. And without the help of the body the mind cannot go as far as it should."

Fun Facts

When he was six years old, Teddy witnessed Abraham Lincoln's funeral procession as it moved through New York City.

Teddy didn't like the sound of that. So he worked hard to get himself into better shape. He followed a daily set of exercises. He started lifting weights.

Teddy also learned to box. He learned to take a hit. And he learned to hit back.

Fun Facts

Teddy and his father actually had a gym built in their house for Teddy to exercise in.

Teddy as a boxer, 1880

Teddy was very serious about heading to the Dakota Territory to hunt **bison**. But he didn't know much about them. Since bison were big, he figured they should be easy to find.

But the Dakota Territory was bigger. Teddy and his guide had a hard time finding any bison at all. It was a land, he wrote, "of vast silent places."

Fun Facts

By the time Teddy was hunting for bison many of the vast herds that had existed only a few decades earlier had already been wiped out.

Putting Down Roots

Teddy's interest in animals went far beyond hunting them. He had always been fascinated by creatures—from the smallest bugs to the biggest elephants.

When he was seven years old, he had seen a dead seal at a local market. He considered himself extremely lucky when he was given the head to bring home a few days later.

Fun Facts

With the seal's head as its centerpiece, Teddy and two of his cousins started what they called the "Roosevelt Museum of Natural History."

Teddy returned to the Dakota Territory several times over the next few years. He built two cattle ranches and worked hard trying to make them a success.

Teddy didn't duck any responsibilities on the ranch. He practiced roping and **branding** cows. If a ditch needed digging, he picked up a shovel. If a fireplace needed wood, he grabbed an axe.

Fun Facts

North and South Dakota both became states on November 2, 1889.

He breathed plenty of trail dust moving his herds from one watering hole to another.

And while Teddy never rode a horse as easily as someone who was born in the saddle, he never refused to ride a horse—even if it looked wild and likely to throw him. He was never afraid to take his chances.

Fun Facts

One of Teddy's ranches, the Elkhorn Ranch, covered 218 acres (88 hectares). Today it is part of the Little Missouri National Grassland.

Aiming to Fit in

When Teddy wasn't taking care of his cattle, he went hunting. As the years passed, he hunted everything from antelope and elk to ducks and rabbits.

Whatever he shot, he skinned and **dressed** the meat to prepare it for eating.

Fun Facts

As a boy, Teddy had learned how to mount and stuff small animals for his collection.

One time, Teddy even faced a grizzly bear. It was 9 feet (2.7 meters) tall and weighed more than 1,000 pounds (454 kilograms). He shot it "right through the brain," the best place to shoot it to make sure the grizzly didn't have him for lunch.

Fun Facts

Teddy Roosevelt never shot at a person until he was a soldier in the Spanish-American War in 1898.

Taking Charge

However, sometimes other dangers crossed his path. Teddy also served as a deputy sheriff in his county. When three thieves stole a boat from his Elkhorn Ranch and headed downriver, Teddy acted at once.

He gathered up a small **posse** of two men whom he described as "tough, hardy, resolute fellows, quick as cats, strong as bears, and able to travel like bull moose."

They trailed the thieves for three days. Teddy was hoping to avoid a shootout, but it was hard to know what would happen next.

Fun Facts

The largest grizzly bear ever measured weighed more than 1,200 pounds (544 kilograms).

The thieves were sharing a campsite, but they had split up when Teddy and his men arrived. One at a time, they surrendered rather than risk being shot.

It took a few days more for Teddy and the others to retrace their steps, but they were able at last to deliver the thieves to jail.

Fun Facts

Teddy and his posse had to build a new boat to follow the thieves on the river because Teddy's boat had been the only one in the area.

Teddy's time in the Wild West stood in sharp contrast to his life back in New York City, where he was beginning a career in politics.

Still, it was the place he declared where "the romance of my life began."

Fun Facts

Although he had spent years out west in the mid 1880s, after 1887 Teddy only returned to the west a few times.

President Theodore Roosevelt

Vice President Theodore "Teddy" Roosevelt became the youngest ever president of the United States in 1901, when at age 42 he succeeded William McKinley, who had been assassinated. Before that, his positions had included being Governor of New York and New York City's Police Commissioner.

As president, Roosevelt built on his experiences out west to establish five national parks and 150 national forests, among other **preserves**. *In October 1918, just three months before his death at age 60, he said in a speech in North Dakota, "I owe more to the times when I lived out here and worked with the men who have been my friends than to anything else."*

GLOSSARY

bison
A wild ox with shaggy hair and a humped back

branding
The act of using a red-hot iron rod to mark cattle as belonging to a particular ranch

city slicker
A sophisticated person from a city who, when visiting a country setting, may want to take advantage of the people who live there

dressed
To clean and season raw meat to prepare it for cooking

lasso
A long rope with a noose at one end used to catch cattle or horses

posse
A group of men who are asked by a sheriff to help hunt down a criminal

preserves
Areas where nature, such as animals and plants, is protected

Wild West
The western United States in the past when there were many cowboys and outlaws

INDEX

COMPREHENSION QUESTIONS

What was the name of the territory that Teddy explored?

How tall was the grizzly bear that Teddy killed?

What did the thieves steal from Teddy?

ABOUT THE AUTHOR

Stephen Krensky is the award-winning author of more than 150 fiction and nonfiction books for children. He and his wife Joan live in Lexington, Massachusetts, and he happily spends as much time as possible with his grown children and not-so-grown grandchildren.

CRABTREE Publishing Company

Written by: Stephen Krensky
Illustrations by: Bobbie Houser
Art direction and layout by: Bobbie Houser
Series Development: James Earley
Proofreader: Petrice Custance
Educational Consultant: Marie Lemke M.Ed.
Print Coordinator: Katherine Berti

Photographs: t = Top, c = Center, b = Bottom, l = Left, r = Right
Alamy: Everett Collection: pp. 12 t, 17 t; Smith Collection/Gado: p. 16 t; Granger: pp. 5 c, 11 tr; Shutterstock: Vorobiov Oleksii 8: cover tl; Everett Collection: cover bl, pp. 4, 9 l, tr, 22 l, 23 tl, tr, br, 28 t, b, 29 b; SchubPhoto: cover br; stockphoto-graf: p. 5 t; Michael Hinkle: pp. 5 b, 22 r; Awesome_art_Creation: p. 7 l; Pavel Smolyakov: p. 7 r; Vracovska: p. 9 br; alexblacksea: p. 10; lynea: p. 11 bl; Dsoto: p. 11 br; Elena Pimonova: p. 12 b; Anh Luu: p. 13 tl; EugenP: p. 13 tr; Tom Reichner: p. 13 b; Anthony Smith Images: p. 15 t; Mikadun: p. 15 bl; Zhivova: p. 15 br; beodra: p. 16 b; Canicula: p. 17 bl; mishu: p. 17 br; Tancha: p. 18; Zack Frank: p. 19 t, bl; Geoffrey Kuchera: p. 19 c; Ken Wolter: p. 19 br; mamita: pp. 20, 21 br; DedMityay: p. 21 tl; Viktoriia Kotliarchuk: p. 21 tr; Norenko Andrey: p. 21 cr; wolfman57: p. 21 bl; HiSunnySky: p. 23 bl; Oleg Iatsun: p. 24; Dennis W Donohue: p. 25 b; Chinch: p. 25 br; val lawless: p. 26; mishu: p. 27 tl; alessandro guerriero: p. 27 tr; LHF Graphics: p. 27 c; Ok Pen: p. 27 b; Roberto Castillo: p. 29 t

Library and Archives Canada Cataloguing in Publication

Available at the Library and Archives Canada

Library of Congress Cataloging-in-Publication Data

Available at the Library of Congress

Crabtree Publishing Company

www.crabtreebooks.com 1-800-387-7650

In Canada: We acknowledge the financial support of the Government of Canada through the Canada Book Fund for our publishing activities.

Published in the United States
Crabtree Publishing
347 Fifth Avenue
Suite 1402-145
New York, NY, 10016

Published in Canada
Crabtree Publishing
616 Welland Ave.
St. Catharines, ON
L2M 5V6

Printed in the U.S.A./072022/CG20220201